GRILLED CHEESE & BEER

RECIPES FOR THE FINER THINGS IN LIFE

KEVIN VANBLARCUM & JAMES EDWARD DAVIS

Hatherleigh Press is committed to preserving and protecting the natural resources of the earth. Environmentally responsible and sustainable practices are embraced within the company's mission statement.

Visit us at www.hatherleighpress.com and register online for free offers, discounts, special events, and more.

GRILLED CHEESE & BEER

Library of Congress Cataloging-in-Publication

Data is available upon request.

ISBN: 978-1-57826-653-1

COVER AND INTERIOR DESIGN BY CAROLYN KASPER

PHOTOGRAPHY BY DYLAN TUCKER

Printed in the United States

10 9 8 7 6 5 4 3 2

This book is dedicated to all of our friends, family, and loved ones. All of the people who, when we told them we wanted to write a book on grilled cheese and beer, laughed *with* us and not *at* us.

Kevin: Thank you to my family and friends; most importantly, thank you to Cassie and Egg. You've made all of this possible.

Eddie: To my father James Kelly Davis Jr., my uncle Vance Fort, and my mother Jeanette Doddy Davis.

CONTENTS

INTRODUCTION

Welcome to *Grilled Cheese & Beer*. If you've come to have this book in your possession, it might be your 21st birthday. Maybe you've just moved into your first apartment. Or maybe you're just a connoisseur of well-crafted culinary tomes. Regardless, we welcome you and we hope you're as excited as we are to go on this gooey and effervescent adventure. However, for that to happen, we might need to prep you on how this book happened and what we are all about.

This book started as a joke. Eddie and I used to make jokes about working at my future fictional (but still completely possible) restaurant "Cheesy Beerds." As you can probably tell, we have been big fans of puns right from the beginning. This hypothetical brewpub/grilled cheese shop prompted us to start developing a fictitious menu, comprised of some hilariously named sandwiches we'd been coming up with (at least, we thought they were hilarious). Hilarious enough to be in a book? Maybe. Crazily enough, we met a publisher who thought so, too. A few different ideas came to mind. 'Dillas and Daquiris. Wine and Wieners (everybody knows wine goes well with hotdogs). When the pure novelty of the whole thing wore off, we realized exactly what we wanted to make a book about and how special this project could be. So, we went to work. Eddie on the sandwich designing vocals, and myself on the beer pairing drums.

Grilled cheese and beer. Needless to say, we feel very passionate about these things. For us, cheese and beer make the world go 'round. I make my living off of brewing beer, and Eddie spends his days whipping up outrageously delicious sandwiches and other foodstuffs. We believe in making these sandwiches into more than just college dorm room fodder. They're an American classic, updated for a foodie dominated era.

Not only do we aim to elevate the grilled cheese, but we want to give it a companion. A best friend. A comrade. A brother in arms. A parter in crime. A pairing worthy of the perfection that is melty cheese slapped between two delicious pieces of perfectly toasted bread. And that is the malty, citrusy, piney, chocolaty, fruity, sour, dry goodness that is the immensely varied selection of beers now available to everyone. There is something for everyone and everything. Every cheese and ingredient combo has a perfect beer out there to send it over the top. We took on this arduous task—it simply had to be done. So we did the research, crunched the numbers and—not to toot our own horn—we nailed it. Now, without further ado, we give you our masterpiece. Our piece de resistance.

PINTS AND PUNGENT PUNS

Puns are hilarious. In fact, we find them to be *so* much fun that we've based our whole book on them. Nothing is more rewarding for us than coming up with a media reference-induced pun and then reverse engineering it into a delicious treat. It's kind of the whole point here.

To be completely honest, our sense of humor is probably pretty corny. And seeing as how this book is an extension of our very beings, it, too, is probably a bit on the corny side. But for us, that's what's so amazing. We go through our daily lives spewing puns and babbling about movies. So it seemed only natural to let this book just be us.

So what makes a good pun? We're not really sure. Some people would argue that "never been cheddar" is not a terribly good one. They might say it's lazy or self-indulgent. We say it's awesome and totally rad. For us, puns are mostly just about owning it—being proud of who you are and letting that freak flag fly. We're nerds who love puns. But we also just wrote a book on grilled cheese and beer. What have *you* done lately?

#Grilledcheesedreamz

THE BEER GUIDE

This is not a beer book. This is a book *involving* beer. We're not looking to teach a new generation of beer snobs the difference between an American sour and a gose; that's just not what this is about. Don't get us wrong, we love the stuff. But this book is about how well beer can enhance a meal of gluten and dairy—namely, grilled cheese. Our guide will cover basics about styles, without delving too deeply into history or science. You'll know your ales from your lagers and your IPAs from your Hefeweizens, and really, that's enough. Beer doesn't have to be a complicated, sophisticated thing (although it often is). It can be fun and refreshing, light and hoppy, bold and malty, citrusy or chocolaty. Beer is broad. Like cheese, it can change dramatically with just a very slight variation. For example, a change in carbonation (the amount of bubbles that are in the beer) can make an enormous difference. A simple change from the more traditional CO_2 to nitrogen changes the beer completely, giving it a thicker texture (as with Guinness) and a creamier mouth feel. This comes from the smaller bubbles. Similarly, a slight change in recipe can make for a complexly different final product. And that's why it's so fun. It's always evolving.

KEY TERMS

IBUs: International bitterness unit.

Malt bill: The combination of different grains used in a recipe.

Mouth feel: Different beers have varying amounts of effervescence. This leads to a variance in how the beer feels when you drink it.

Nitro: Refers to a beer made with nitrogen instead of CO_2. This gives the beer a creamier mouth feel (the best example of this is Guinness).

Session: An IPA that is 4% or lower. These beers are sessionable, or drinkable.

ALES VS LAGERS

Essentially, beer can be broken into two categories: ales and lagers. It all comes down to the yeast that's used. Ales, which ferment at warmer temperatures, are top-fermenting beers. The more common varieties of ales include pale ale, Hefeweizen, and IPA (India pale ale). The yeasts are varied and abundant.

Lagers, which ferment at colder temperatures, are bottom-fermenting beers. Originally, lagers were beers that would be stored in caves outside of the German town of Einbech. (In fact, even the word "lager" comes from the German word meaning "to store".) Lagers typically take longer to ferment, so they would leave their beers in the caves for long periods of time. Lagers are the most popular beers in the world. Being that lagers are defined by their light, crisp flavors and slow fermenting process, there is not a lot of variety within the style. As such, lagers make up but a small yet significant part of the beer spectrum. They are generally light in color and fairly low on the hop spectrum. Their crisp and refreshing nature has made them the most drinkable beers on the planet. From Coors to Budweiser to Heineken, they all use lager yeast.

ALES

PALE ALE: The pale ale is your typical ale. Characterized by a nice balance of malt and hops, it can often vary in flavor. It can be characterized by its relatively light color.

IPA (INDIA PALE ALE): The India pale ale is known for its use of hops. These are typically bitter but can often take on other hop characteristics, such as pine, citrus, and floral aromas. Hops have oils that help preserve the beer and prevent it from going bad for a much longer period of time. During earlier colonization, this ensured that the beer could make it to England's colonies without spoiling.

HEFEWEIZEN/WHEAT BEER: These beers are different by virtue of the fact that their malt bill, or grain recipe, is mostly wheat. They often take on fruity notes of banana and clove.

STOUTS: Dark and full bodied. These often have notes of coffee, chocolate, and roasted barley.

PORTER: Similar to a stout, although the recipes often lack some of the roasted barleys that are in stouts. They have history in industrial England and tend to be more aggressively hopped.

LAGERS

PILSNER: Like most lagers, they're crisp and refreshing. Characterized by its light color and body, with a slight hop character. They'll quench your thirst.

AMERICAN LAGERS: Budweiser and Coors. 'Nuff said.

BOCK: Bock beers are lagers that have been made with darker malt bills. Typically stronger in nature, these are in the vein of the first lagers to be made.

There are an almost infinite number of beer styles nowadays. Imperial (strong) extra coffee porter. East coast copper IPA. Cherry Rhubarb Sour. West coast tropical hoppy pilsner. Having a general knowledge will prepare you to survive at your local beer distributor. Don't let the wacky descriptions intimidate you. Beer people just like to write and want to show you how clever they are. Trust me—I'm one of them.

THE CHEESE GUIDE

heese, like beer, isn't overly complicated. We're definitely not experts on the subject, but we do eat a hell of a lot of the stuff.
Here's what we've learned along the way.

CHEDDAR

Cheddar comes in tons of varieties. It's a hard cheese that often has a bite to it. It melts reasonably well and will pretty much make anything taste better. Some of our favorites are horseradish cheddar, Adirondack cheddar, and jalapeño cheddar.

MUENSTER

This semi-soft cheese often takes on whatever flavors are added to it. It melts really well and goes nicely with most other ingredients. Some of our favorites are jalapeño Muenster, dill Muenster, and three pepper Muenster.

GOUDA

This is a harder cheese that, like cheddar, comes in many varieties. We like the pesto Gouda ourselves. Plus, when you use it you can tell your friends to "have a Gouda day." That alone seems worth it to us.

BRIE

Brie is soft and often bland. For a lot of folks, it's a texture thing. It will pretty much take on whatever flavors are added to it. The rind also holds some unique flavor characteristics. Being that it is the part of the cheese which comes in contact with mold, it often carries a "mushroomy" or earthy flavor.

COLBY JACK

Colby is usually just found on a cracker taken from a cheese plate. We believed in it, though. It melts reasonably well and is mild enough to let other flavors shine. Plus, Colby jack is just straight up delicious.

PROVOLONE

Provolone is probably America's favorite lunch cheese. Everybody eats this stuff. It's not super overpowering, but it can pack a nice smoky flavor. It goes well with most meats.

CREAM CHEESE

We don't feel the need to describe this one, but that seems rude. Cream cheese is a flavorful soft cheese that is amazing for bonding ingredients as well as complementing them with its tangy notes. Always a welcome ingredient.

HAVARTI

This cheese is super soft and melts amazingly. It's great when made with dill, jalapeños, or pesto.

GOAT CHEESE

Goat cheese is soft and packed with flavor. You can usually find them with some crazy flavor additions, but the honey variety is the most nuanced and well balanced in our opinion.

Any of these cheese can be found at most grocery stores in many, many varieties. Go out and search. You never know when you might find a sweet dill Havarti or honey goat cheese. Cheeses are one of the rare things in the world that pretty much go with everything. We're pretty sure there should be a religion just about cheese.

RECIPES

hhh…we've made it. After a long lead-up (that most people will probably have skipped over, despite our hard work), we've made it. This is why you're here, after all. We've broken the recipes up by skill level to ensure that you don't get in over your head. So use the system! Seriously. You're not ready for the crazy stuff yet.

Don't believe us? Then go ahead. We dare you.

Oh, and remember these two tidbits:

1 The universal first step for making a great grilled cheese sandwich is to grease the bread. You can spread butter or mayo on one side of the bread, dealer's choice.

2 By all means, feel free to add tomato, bacon, onions…oh hell, add anything you want to whatever sandwich you want. It's important to remember that you're the one eating it.

Enjoy!

THE BASICS

A GOOD PLACE TO START

THE USUAL SUSPECTS

2 slices white bread

4 slices yellow American cheese

3 medium tomato slices

3 strips bacon

STEP 1: Grease one side of each slice of bread and place in a pan on medium heat, greased side down.

STEP 2: Place the cheese on the bread so that all of the bread is covered.

STEP 3: Once the cheese is melted, put tomato on one piece of bread and bacon on the other.

STEP 4: Put both slices of cheesy goodness together and consume.

PAIRING

A simple grilled cheese calls for a simple companion. A traditional American pale ale will complement these simple and delicious classics perfectly. For those interested in lighter fare, **Rolling Rock Extra Pale** will allow these subdued ingredients to shine, while a slightly hoppier **Brooklyn East India Pale Ale** will loudly complement the bacon flavor.

NEVER BEEN CHEDDAR

2 slices sour dough bread
2 slices sharp cheddar cheese
1 slice Adirondack cheddar cheese
1 slice jalapeño cheddar
   (or your favorite cheddar)

STEP 1: Grease one side of each slice of bread and place in a pan on medium heat, greased side down.

STEP 2: Place your assorted cheddars on the bread so that all of the bread is covered.

STEP 3: When the cheese is all nice and melty, put bread together and enjoy.

PAIRING

Cheddar is loud and delicious, sharp and spicy. Any session IPA (low in alcohol) will do. You want to allow the cheddars to show through on their own, without being overpowered. For this, you're going to want to look for a more floral IPA in the range of about 45 IBUs so it has a balanced finish. **Founder's All Day IPA** fits the billing and will ensure that your lunch experience has "never been cheddar."

LIARS GRILLED CHEESE (IT'S FULL OF BOLOGNA)

2 slices white bread
4 slices yellow American cheese
3 slices bologna

STEP 1: Grease one side of each slice of bread and place in a pan on medium heat, greased side down.

STEP 2: Place the cheese on the bread so that all of the bread is covered.

STEP 3: In a separate pan, lightly grill the bologna.

STEP 4: Put the lightly grilled bologna on the cheese.

STEP 5: Once the cheese is all ooey-gooey, put the bread together and enjoy your Liars Grilled Cheese.

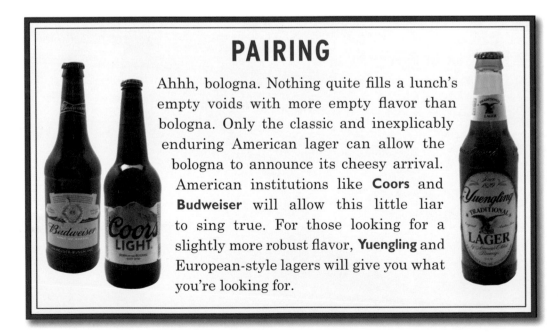

PAIRING

Ahhh, bologna. Nothing quite fills a lunch's empty voids with more empty flavor than bologna. Only the classic and inexplicably enduring American lager can allow the bologna to announce its cheesy arrival. American institutions like **Coors** and **Budweiser** will allow this little liar to sing true. For those looking for a slightly more robust flavor, **Yuengling** and European-style lagers will give you what you're looking for.

JACK OF ALL TRADES

2 slices wheat bread

2 slices Colby jack cheese

2 Monterey jack cheese

2 slices pepper jack cheese

2 slices tomato

3 slices onion

* Feel free to experiment with
whatever jack cheese you can find.

STEP 1: Grease one side of each slice of bread and place in a pan on medium heat, greased side down.

STEP 2: Place the cheese on the bread so that all of the bread is covered.

STEP 3: When cheese is melted, put on tomatoes and onions.

STEP 4: Put bread together and enjoy.

PAIRING

Jack cheese is a tricky thing. Sweet or spicy, this one can do it all. Colby jack and Monterey jack will lend themselves to a sweeter beer like a **Hoegaarden** or a malty Bock. For those adding a pepper or jalapeño jack, go for something higher in IBUs. Depending on the cheese, **Ithaca Beer Company's Flower Power** or a **Sierra Nevada IPA** should do the trick.

JOHNNY APPLE CHEESE

2 slices whole grain bread
4 slices Adirondack cheddar cheese
1 granny smith apple
3 strips bacon

STEP 1: Grease one side of each slice of bread and place in a pan on medium heat, greased side down.

STEP 2: Place the cheddar on the bread so that all of the bread is covered.

STEP 3: Thinly slice the granny smith apple and place it on one slice of bread so the cheese and bread is completely covered.

STEP 4: Add bacon strips to other slice of bread and cheese.

STEP 5: Once the cheese is melted, put the sandwich together and *tada*! You are all set.

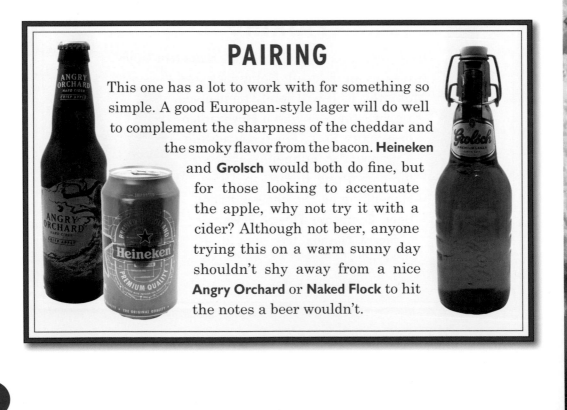

PAIRING

This one has a lot to work with for something so simple. A good European-style lager will do well to complement the sharpness of the cheddar and the smoky flavor from the bacon. **Heineken** and **Grolsch** would both do fine, but for those looking to accentuate the apple, why not try it with a cider? Although not beer, anyone trying this on a warm sunny day shouldn't shy away from a nice **Angry Orchard** or **Naked Flock** to hit the notes a beer wouldn't.

THE BEE'S KNEES

1 English muffin
3 thin slices honey ham
2 slices mild cheddar cheese
Honey, to drizzle

STEP 1: Toast the English muffin to your liking.

STEP 2: Lightly grill the ham in a pan on medium heat.

STEP 3: Place the cheddar on both halves of the English muffin and place the grilled ham on the cheddar.

STEP 4: Place both halves of the English muffin in a toaster oven or oven at 350°F for 2–4 minutes or until the cheese is melted.

STEP 5: Remove the English muffin from the oven and lightly drizzle honey over both halves.

STEP 6: Put the halves together and *bam, zoom, straight to the moon* you got yourself a Bee's Knees.

PAIRING

As one of our breakfast offerings, this one calls for something delicious and hearty. However, like any good breakfast, this means many options. A **Blue Moon** with an orange wedge is never going to let you down, but for those craving something a little more filling, a heavy oatmeal or brunch stout will help the ham and honey to shine. **Samuel Smith's Oatmeal Stout** will really turn this one into the Bee's Knees.

MUENSTER MASH

¼ yellow onion

2 slices white bread

2 slices Muenster cheese

2 slices jalapeño Muenster cheese

STEP 1: Slice the onion into thin slices and sauté until clear.

STEP 2: Grease one side of each slice of bread and place in a pan on medium heat, greased side down.

STEP 3: Place the cheese on the bread so that all of the bread is covered.

STEP 4: When the cheese is nice and melty, put both pieces together and enjoy the Muenster Mash—it *is* a graveyard smash.

PAIRING

Muenster, like Colby, can hop all over the flavor spectrum. Delicious on its own and with spices, it really adopts flavors and makes them into some sort of frankencheesebeer monster. Any European-style lager with some hop character will work nicely here. **Stella Artois** falls into this category; however, someone with the means should try to track down **Rothaus**. This southern German beer has just the right balance to turn this run of the mill pitchfork mob into the Muenster Mash you need.

NOT YOUR DAD'S FRIED BOLOGNA

7 slices bologna

2 slices potato bread

4 slices provolone cheese

2 slices onion

Spoonful of relish

STEP 1: Fry the bologna in a pan.

STEP 2: Grease the bread and place in a pan, and then cover with provolone.

STEP 3: Place the fried bologna on both sides of the bread.

STEP 4: Lightly spread onion and relish on one side of the bread.

STEP 5: When the cheese is melted, put both halves together.

PAIRING

We all have that one person in our life. That one person who just refuses to get on board with eating bologna sandwiches. This particular pairing is an ode to my fiancé's father who had us make a special bologna sandwich while coming up with recipes. In order to make this one extra awesome, try it with a refreshing lager. **Modelo Especial** is preferred, but **Negra Modelo** will give you the little bit of extra flavor you might be looking for.

TURKEY IN THE RYE

2 slices rye bread
4 slices Swiss cheese
⅓ pound turkey
2 scallions, chopped
Thousand Island dressing, to drizzle

STEP 1: Grease the bread and place in a pan, and then cover with the Swiss cheese.

STEP 2: In a separate pan, grill the turkey and chopped scallions.

STEP 3: Drizzle Thousand Island dressing on one half of the bread.

STEP 4: When the cheese is melted, put the grilled turkey and scallions on the cheese.

STEP 5: Put both halves together and enjoy.

PAIRING

Even Holden Caulfield couldn't complain about this one. Although (like any good beer snob), he'd find something wrong with drinking a typical American lager to complement this fancy sandy. Instead, try it with something a little darker, like a nice light (in body) stout. **Keegan Ales' Mother's Milk** and **Left Hand Brewing's Milk Stout** will both make this combo a hit, just like Salinger's 1951 emotional rollercoaster.

THE BLUE AU JUS

2 slices pumpernickel bread

4 ounces blue cheese chunk

3 slices American cheese

⅓ pound roast beef

1 small bowl au jus dip*

*To make an easy au jus, mix beef base
   paste with water and boil.

STEP 1: Grease the bread and place in a pan, and then spread blue cheese on top and cover with American cheese.

STEP 2: In a separate pan, lightly grill the roast beef.

STEP 3: Put the roast beef on the cheese.

STEP 4: When the cheese is melted, put the sandwich together and give it a dunk in your au jus. Take a bite and let the Blue Au Jus wash over you.

PAIRING

These are some bold flavors. Go for something fairly high in the IBUs department. **Founder's All Day IPA** session will complement it nicely without overpowering the flavors.

THE BRUCE LEROY

2 slices rye bread
4 slices Havarti cheese
⅓ pound roasted pork
Handful of sauerkraut
Handful of fried onions
Dijon mustard, to drizzle

STEP 1: Grease the bread and place in a pan, and then cover with the Havarti.

STEP 2: In a separate pan, fry the pork, sauerkraut, and onions.

STEP 3: Drizzle Dijon mustard over the cheese.

STEP 4: Put the pork and sauerkraut onto the cheese.

STEP 5: Close up the sandwich and take a bite of the last dragon of sandwiches, the Bruce Leroy.

PAIRING

Any bold German pilsner will pair nicely. **Hofbräu Pilsner** will always go well with pork and sauerkraut, but anyone who can find **Veltins** or **Radeberger** won't be disappointed.

THE SEA BISCUIT

1 English muffin
¼ pound roast beef
2 slices edam Swiss cheese
Horseradish, to drizzle

STEP 1: Cut the English muffin in half and put into the toaster to lightly toast.

STEP 2: Cover both halves of the English muffing with Swiss cheese and put into an oven at 350°F.

STEP 3: In a pan, lightly grill the roast beef but try not to over-grill it.

STEP 4: When the cheese is melted on the English muffin, take it out of the oven and drizzle horseradish over the cheese.

STEP 5: Put the roast beef onto the cheese and put both halves of sandwich together. Saddle up for the Sea Biscuit.

PAIRING

New Belgium's Fat Tire amber ale will have you *neighing* in disbelief. Light enough to let the sandwich shine, yet bold enough to win the flavor race… just like Tobey Maguire did.

CHEEZUS CRUST

1 hot cross bun

4 thin slices Swiss cheese

¼ avocado

2 slices bacon

Tuna salad, to taste

STEP 1: Slice the bun in half, cover with Swiss cheese, and place in an oven or toaster oven at 350°F.

STEP 2: Once the cheese is melted, take the bun out of the oven.

STEP 3: Put the tuna salad, avocado, and bacon on the bun.

STEP 4: Put the whole thing together and prepare for a religious experience.

PAIRING

Ahhh, Swiss. The holiest of cheeses. There's really not much to this one. It has earthy flavors that meld super well, so go for something sweet and malty. **Newcastle Brown Ale** will pair nicely, but if you're looking to strictly complement the motif, **The Black Sheep Brewery** makes a Monty Python-themed **Holy Grail Ale** that would do nicely.

MÉNAGE À CINQ

3 slices sourdough bread
2 slices cheddar cheese
1 slice mozzarella cheese
1 slice Muenster cheese
1 slice pepper jack cheese
1 slice provolone cheese
¼ avocado

STEP 1: Grease one side of each slice of bread and place in a pan on medium heat, greased side down.

STEP 2: Cover all three slices with cheese (in no particular order).

STEP 3: Once the cheese is melted, put avocado on two slices.

STEP 4: Slap it together and take a step into the Ménage à Cinq.

PAIRING

This is our ode to one of our favorite shows, "The League." Except instead of it being Andre's swanky wine bar, it's a delicious sandwich paired with a light refreshing lager—one with some punch behind it. **Otter Creek's Citra Mantra** is a pretty good bet if you can find it. If not, the guys on the show always prefer **Stella Artois** or **Bud Light**. Old post office boxes are a pretty sweet idea for a bar, though. Right?

BICYCLE THIEVES

1 bâtard
4 slices pepper jack cheese
2 roasted red pepper halves
⅓ pound hot capicola
Pinch of sprouts
Handful of arugula

STEP 1: Slice the bâtard in half and put the pepper jack on both halves.

STEP 2: On the bottom half of the bread, put the red peppers on, and then put both halves in an oven at 350°F.

STEP 3: In a pan, lightly grill the capicola.

STEP 4: Once the cheese is melted on the bâtard, take it out of the oven and put the sprouts and arugula on the red peppers, then put the capicola on top of that.

STEP 5: Put the sandwich together, slice it up, call some friends, and enjoy.

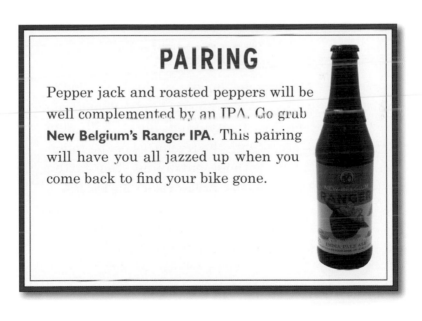

PAIRING

Pepper jack and roasted peppers will be well complemented by an IPA. Go grub **New Belgium's Ranger IPA**. This pairing will have you all jazzed up when you come back to find your bike gone.

49

FOR YOUR FERNGULLET

1 tomato, cut into quarters

2 mushrooms, rough cut

2 slices potato bread

4 slices smoked mozzarella cheese

STEP 1: In a pan, add tomatoes and mushrooms and fry until both are soft.

STEP 2: Grease one side of each slice of bread and place in a pan on medium heat, greased side down. Place the mozzarella on the bread so that all of the bread is covered.

STEP 3: Put the tomatoes and mushrooms onto the mozzarella.

STEP 4: Once the cheese is melted, put the sandwich together and imagine you're in the last rainforest.

PAIRING

Mushrooms make us think of "FernGully." We're nineties kids! Something earthy, fruity, and floral will help accentuate the freshness of the tomatoes without outshining the earthy mushrooms. **Ballast Point's Big Eye IPA** is just as complex as FernGully seemed to me at five years old. So drink it and watch it. Respectively, of course.

ADVANCED

YOU'VE GOT A GRASP ON CHEESE AND BREAD

THE FRENCH CONNECTION

½ baguette

5 slices Brie

1 spoonful tart cherry jam (or whatever type of jam or jelly you prefer, if cherry isn't your scene)

3 ounces shredded Gruyère cheese

STEP 1: Slice the baguette in half lengthwise.

STEP 2: Thinly slice the Brie and place across both halves of the bread.

STEP 3: Place both halves into an oven or toaster oven at 350°F degrees for 2–3 minutes, until the Brie starts melting.

STEP 4: Remove the baguette from the oven and lightly spread tart cherry jam over the Brie.

STEP 5: Shred the Gruyère with a grater and lightly sprinkle over the Brie and jam.

STEP 6: Place the baguette back in the oven for 1–2 minutes, or until the Gruyère is melted.

STEP 7: Remove from the oven, combine, slice the baguette, and enjoy. (This is great to have with a couple of friends.)

PAIRING

France is known for wine, not beer. It's a shame, really. Those who have had a true Biere de Garde know that it takes your taste buds on a car chase to rival a certain 1971 Gene Hackman classic. For those of us who find these franc treasures hard to come by, any malty bock or Oktoberfest will do the trick. **Celebrator** is well-known for a reason, but **Samuel Adams' Octoberfest** is no slouch.

JACK AND DILL

2 spears asparagus

6 slices cucumber

2 slices wheat bread

2 slices Colby jack cheese

2 slices dill Havarti cheese

STEP 1: Cut the asparagus spears in half and steam in a pan until tender, then slice the cucumber into thin slices.

STEP 2: Grease one side of each slice of bread and place in a pan on medium heat, greased side down.

STEP 3: Place the Colby jack on one slice of bread and the dill Havarti on the other.

STEP 4: When the cheese is nice and melty, put the cucumber slices on one half and the steamed asparagus on the other.

STEP 5: Put both halves together and take your jack and dill up the hill and fetch a pail of beer.

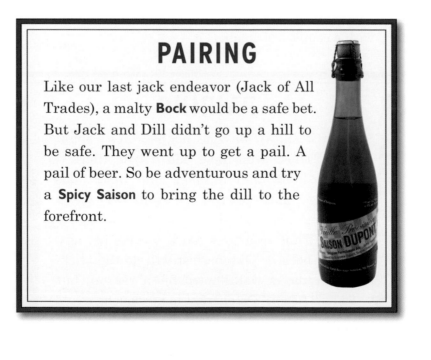

PAIRING

Like our last jack endeavor (Jack of All Trades), a malty **Bock** would be a safe bet. But Jack and Dill didn't go up a hill to be safe. They went up to get a pail. A pail of beer. So be adventurous and try a **Spicy Saison** to bring the dill to the forefront.

HOGS AND HOLES

4 thin slices roast pork

2 slices rye bread

4 slices Swiss cheese

1 dill pickle spear

STEP 1: In a pan, lightly grill the pork.

STEP 2: Grease one side of each slice of bread and place in a pan on medium heat, greased side down.

STEP 3: Lay the Swiss cheese over the bread so that all of the bread is completely covered.

STEP 4: On one slice of bread, put the grilled pork.

STEP 5: Slice the pickle in half and place both halves on one slice of bread.

STEP 6: When the cheese is melted, put both halves together and enjoy.

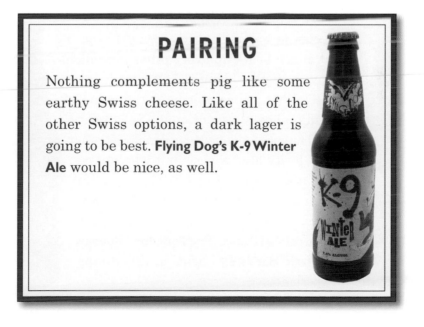

PAIRING

Nothing complements pig like some earthy Swiss cheese. Like all of the other Swiss options, a dark lager is going to be best. **Flying Dog's K-9 Winter Ale** would be nice, as well.

BLACK AND BLUE

2 slices pumpernickel bread
4 slices American cheese
2 slices bacon
Blue cheese, to taste

STEP 1: Grease one side of each slice of bread and place in a pan on medium heat, greased side down.

STEP 2: Place the American cheese on the bread so that all of the bread is covered.

STEP 3: Crumble the blue cheese and spread over the American cheese.

STEP 4: When the cheese is melted, put the bacon on the cheese, then put both halves together and enjoy.

PAIRING

Blue cheese has an overpowering flavor. It pretty much beats up every other ingredient when it comes to being the star, so it takes a special beer to complement that kind of attention hog. Conventional wisdom says bold flavors will overpower and restrain that feisty blue cheese, but why not go the other way? Fruit beers have an interesting way of soothing the savage beast by bringing out the sweetness over the tartness. Try **Founders' Rübæus** or **Magic Hat's #9** to beat up this dining experience.

REVENGE OF THE SWISS

Handful of Swiss chard
2 sliced mushrooms
1 good-sized piece ciabatta bread
4 slices Swiss cheese

STEP 1: In a pan, steam the Swiss chard and mushrooms until tender.

STEP 2: Slice the ciabatta in half and place the Swiss cheese on both sides so that all of the bread is covered.

STEP 3: Put the steamed Swiss chard and mushrooms on the ciabatta.

STEP 4: Place both halves in an oven or toaster oven at 350°F for 4–5 minutes, or until the cheese is melted.

STEP 5: Take both halves out of oven and use the Force to put both together and enjoy the Revenge of the Swiss.

PAIRING

Swiss cheese is nutty. Crazy. Wacky. But mostly, it has as a nutty flavor and is full of holes. Just like the Jedi Order. This is an earthy grilled cheese that needs something malty and refreshing. **Newcastle Brown Ale** is a sure thing, but a schwarzbier like **Krombacher Dark (Schwarz)** or **Samuel Adams' Black Lager** would both do nicely to bring it to the dark side. The Force is strong with this one.

HAMWISE GAMGEE

3 thin slices honey ham
Handful of spinach
2 slices wheat bread
4 slices Havarti cheese
Honey mustard, to drizzle

STEP 1: In a pan, lightly grill the ham.

STEP 2: In another pan, steam the spinach until soft.

STEP 3: Grease one side of each slice of bread and place in a pan on medium heat, greased side down.

STEP 4: Place the Havarti on the bread so that all of the bread is covered.

STEP 5: On one slice of bread, put the grilled ham and on the other, place the steamed spinach.

STEP 6: When the cheese is melted, lightly drizzle honey mustard over the ham.

STEP 7: Now slap it together, Frodo Baggins, and enjoy your Hamwise Gamgee.

PAIRING

This hearty grilled cheese is worthy to be served at the Prancing Pony, something a travel weary wizard might sink their teeth into while they enjoy a nice pint of mead. Naturally, we recommend a honey mead to wash this one down. However, for those of us with a preference for hops over honey, a good IPA will do. **Stone Brewing's** would be particularly yummy. This may not be the one sandwich to rule them all, but it's still pretty damn good.

MAUI WOWI

2 ¼-inch slices Spam
2 pineapple rings
1 Hawaiian roll
4 slices Havarti cheese

STEP 1: Lightly grill both sides of the Spam slices and pineapple rings.

STEP 2: Cut the Hawaiian roll in half and put Havarti on both sides so that all of the bread is covered.

STEP 3: Put the grilled Spam and pineapple rings on both halves of the roll.

STEP 4: Put both halves of the roll in an oven or toaster oven at 350°F for 4–5 minutes, or until the cheese is melted.

STEP 5: Take both halves out of oven, slap 'em together and *wowi*, that's a good Maui Wowi.

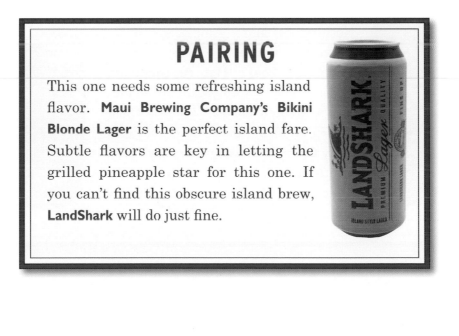

PAIRING

This one needs some refreshing island flavor. **Maui Brewing Company's Bikini Blonde Lager** is the perfect island fare. Subtle flavors are key in letting the grilled pineapple star for this one. If you can't find this obscure island brew, **LandShark** will do just fine.

GRILLED CHEESE (BURGER)

1 6-ounce burger patty
2 slices whole grain bread
2 slices tomato
4 slices American cheese

STEP 1: Grill the burger patty to your liking.

STEP 2: Grease one side of each slice of bread and place in a pan on medium heat, greased side down.

STEP 3: Put the grilled burger on one slice of bread and the tomatoes on the other.

STEP 4: Add cheese on top of both slices.

STEP 5: When the cheese is melted, put both slices together and enjoy.

PAIRING

Nothing is more American than a burger, so it needs a quintessential American beer. **21st Amendment's IPA** is a good complement to a juicy burger grilled cheese, but for those looking to be as 'murican as they can, **Natty Greene's Brewing Company's Freedom American IPA** definitely screams democracy. Or **Genesee's Cream Ale**, just 'cause.

THE GONZO GOUDA

1 ground turkey burger

2 slices potato bread

4 slices chipotle Gouda cheese

Handful of sautéed mushrooms

3 slices pickled beets

Thomas Lumpkin's Sweet and Spicy BBQ Sauce (or your favorite BBQ sauce), to taste

STEP 1: In a pan, fry the turkey burger.

STEP 2: Grease the bread and place in a pan, and then cover with the Gouda.

STEP 3: Butter a separate pan and sauté the chopped mushrooms.

STEP 4: When the turkey burger is done, place on the cheese.

STEP 5: When the mushrooms are done, put them on top of the turkey burger.

STEP 6: On the other piece of bread, lay out the pickled beet slices and drizzle the barbecue sauce

STEP 7: Put the sandwich together, cut in half, take a bite, and roll off into bat country.

PAIRING

Solely because it seems proper, any **Flying Dog** beer will go good with this one. Just look at the labels and you'll get it. In particular, **Old Scratch Amber Lager** will have you full of fear and loathing of how good this combo is.

ICKLE PICKLE

6 slices grilled eggplant

2 slices potato bread

4 slices mozzarella cheese

1 whole pickle spear

STEP 1: Slice the eggplant and lightly grill in a pan.

STEP 2: Grease one side of each slice of bread and place in a pan on medium heat, greased side down.

STEP 3: Put the mozzarella slices on the bread so that all of the bread is covered.

STEP 4: Put the grilled eggplant slices on one slice of bread.

STEP 5: Slice the pickle spear in half and place both halves on the bread.

STEP 6: When the cheese is melted, put both halves of the sandwich together and enjoy.

PAIRING

These are strong flavors—not necessarily bold, but rather sour, sweet, and nuanced. A nice quiet sour beer will do the trick. **Uinta Brewing's Birthday Suit**, although ever changing, is typically pretty spot on. Sours are often hit or miss, so feel free to try as many as you can.

JACK'S WHEATNEY GAINSBOURG

1 wedge brie
2 slices whole grain bread
Spoonful of cranberry sauce
½ avocado
Handful of greens

STEP 1: Slice the brie into six thin slices.

STEP 2: Grease one side of each slice of bread and place in a pan on medium heat, greased side down.

STEP 3: Place the brie on the bread so that all of the bread is covered.

STEP 4: Spread the cranberry sauce on one slice of the bread.

STEP 5: When the brie starts melting, put the slices of avocado on top of the cranberry sauce and put the mixed greens on the other slice.

STEP 6: Put both sides together, put on a Serge Gainsbourg record, and bite into some happiness.

PAIRING

When I was working at The Caboose, me and the owner, Jack, would joke about Whitney Houston and Serge Gainsbourg's extremely awkward conversation on French television. If YouTube had been a thing in the 80's this would have a bazillion hits. It's painful. So since this is one of Jack's creations and since he has been a huge influence and supporter of mine, it only seems right to name this one after Jack and our long-running joke. Thank you, bossman, for everything. These light and frontline flavors are well-balanced and need something fruity yet heavy; something light and citrusy. Any **Hefeweizen** will nail it, but if you can find **Denison's Brewing Company's Weissbier** you won't regret it.

OAKLEY'S BAR AND GRILLED CHEESE

1 good-sized piece ciabatta bread
6 slices mozzarella cheese
Handful of pepperoni
Pinch of crushed red pepper
Spoonful of sun-dried tomato pesto

STEP 1: Cover both halves of the ciabatta with mozzarella.

STEP 2: Spread the pepperoni over the cheese and sprinkle crushed red pepper over the pepperoni.

STEP 3: Place both halves of ciabatta in an oven at 350°F.

STEP 4: When the cheese starts melting, take out one half of the ciabatta and spread on the sun-dried tomato pesto.

STEP 5: Put the ciabatta half back in the oven until the cheese is melted on both halves.

STEP 6: Take the sandwich out of the oven, slice, and enjoy.

PAIRING

Oakley's is one of our favorite local establishments and could probably take a lot of credit as the place where this book became a "thing." As such, drink a beer that's going to be refreshing but won't overpower this pizza-inspired delight. **Keegan Ales' Old Capital** golden ale is a local favorite, but for those of you not on the East Coast, a golden pale ale or lager will do.

THE BIG KAHUNA

¼ pound roasted pork
Handful of fried onions
Teriyaki sauce, to drizzle
Hawaiian roll
2 slices Havarti cheese
2 grilled pineapple rings

STEP 1: In a pan, fry the pork and onions, lightly drizzling teriyaki over both.

STEP 2: On both halves of the Hawaiian roll, put Havarti cheese and place in an oven at 350°F.

STEP 3: When the cheese is melted, take it out of the oven and drizzle teriyaki sauce on the roll.

STEP 4: On the bottom halve of the roll, put the pork and onions mixture. On the top, put the grilled pineapple rings.

STEP 5: Sit down and enjoy your Big Kahuna and wash it down with a refreshing Sprite....

PAIRING

...or a beer. Nice, light, refreshing lagers complement these ingredients really well. But for those of you who might like to stray from the norm, **21st Amendment's Hell or High Watermelon** is just the refreshing wave you need.

THE DILL WEED

2 slices whole grain bread
8 slices dill Havarti cheese
Handful of dandelion greens
Honey, to drizzle

STEP 1: Grease the bread and place in a pan, and then cover with the Havarti.

STEP 2: In another pan, steam the dandelion greens.

STEP 3: Place the steamed greens on one half of the bread.

STEP 4: Lightly drizzle honey over the sandwich.

STEP 5: When the cheese is melted, take it out of the pan and enjoy.

PAIRING

Grassy and spicy. Any session IPA or Pale Ale will accentuate the dill nicely. **Sierra Nevada's Pale Ale** is classic and consistent.

THE EMPIRE STATE GRILLED CHEESE

New York City salt bagel
2 slices Adirondack cheddar cheese
4 slices bacon
4 slices of any New York state apple
Real maple syrup, to drizzle

STEP 1: Cut the bagel in half and grill until light brown.

STEP 2: Cover the bagel with the cheddar and place in an oven at 350°F.

STEP 3: When the cheese starts to melt, put the bacon on the bagel.

STEP 4: When the cheese is melted, take the sandwich out of oven, place apples slices on one side, and drizzle maple syrup over the sandwich.

STEP 5: Put it together and take a bite out of the Big Apple of sandwiches.

PAIRING

Just out of love for my home state, drink some New York beer. **Keegan Ales' Hurricane Kitty** or **Brooklyn Brewery's lager** will both help this one out in different ways. But they'll both keep you in an empire state of mind.

FUNKY BÂTARD

1 French bâtard
½ spoonful ginger spread
6 slices apple
½ avocado
4 slices tomato
4 slices provolone cheese

STEP 1: On both halves of bread, lightly cover with the ginger spread.

STEP 2: On both halves, stack the apple slices, then avocado, tomato, and provolone.

STEP 3: Place both halves in an oven at 350°F until the cheese is melted.

STEP 4: Take out of the oven, combine, and enjoy your sandwich; it is one funky bâtard.

PAIRING

Any kind of Farmhouse Saison will take some bite without sacrificing flavor. **Ommegang Brewery's Hennepin** will do great, but if you're looking for something a little bit more complex try **La Fin du Monde by Unibroue.** This Belgian style will do well to keep things funky.

THE DANGER ERIC

1 piece focaccia bread
4 slices Muenster cheese
1/3 pound chicken
1 rosemary sprig
Handful of arugula
1/4 avocado
Salt and pepper, to taste

STEP 1: Slice the focaccia in half and place in a pan, then cover with the Muenster.

STEP 2: Cut the raw chicken into strips and grill in a pan on medium heat and season with salt, pepper, and rosemary.

STEP 3: When the chicken is cooked, put the chicken on the cheese.

STEP 4: Put a handful of arugula on top of the chicken.

STEP 5: Place the avocado on top of the arugula and chicken.

STEP 6: When the cheese is melted, put the sandwich together and hold on tight for The Danger Eric.

PAIRING

This one is crafted from fine ingredients, just like Clapton's music. It needs something earthy and full in body to complement it nicely. **Rogue's American Amber Ale's** malty notes will sweep you off your feet just like Clapton's tasty licks.

GOOEY LEWIS AND THE BLUES

1 hard roll

8 ounces chunk blue cheese

2 slices cheddar cheese

⅓ pound raw chicken

Handful of spinach

4 cucumber slices

Seasoned salt, to taste

STEP 1: Cut the roll in half and place the blue cheese and cheddar on each half, with blue cheese on top. Put into an oven at 350°F.

STEP 2: Butter a pan and fry the chicken, lightly seasoning with seasoned salt.

STEP 3: In a separate pan, steam the spinach.

STEP 4: When the cheese is melted, take it out of the oven and place the chicken, spinach, and cucumber slices.

STEP 5: Put both halves together, take a bite, and remember the sandwich is Gooey Lewis and you just tasted the Blues.

PAIRING

You've got the *blues*. Blue cheese is strong and pungent, so you need a strong flavorful beer to balance it out. **Dogfish Head's 60 Minute IPA** is just off-center enough to have you feel soulful.

ARTICHOKE BUNKER

2 slices pumpernickel bread

2 slices American cheese

2 slices Swiss cheese

½ pound pastrami

1 spoonful artichoke hearts

2 sun-dried tomatoes

Spicy mayo, to drizzle

STEP 1: Grease the bread and place in a pan, then cover one slice with the American cheese and the other with the Swiss cheese.

STEP 2: In a separate pan, grill the pastrami.

STEP 3: Spread the artichoke heart and sun-dried tomatoes on both slices of bread.

STEP 4: Put the grilled pastrami on the bread.

STEP 5: Drizzle spicy mayo over the pastrami.

STEP 6: Sit down in your favorite chair and take a bite, Meathead.

PAIRING

We're not sure what kind of beer Archie Bunker would be into, but what we do know is a saison will go perfectly with this. Pastrami needs some kind of spicy beer to balance it out. **Allagash Brewing Company** and **Stone Brewing Company** both make very suitable saisons that'll make you feel like you're at 704 Hauser Street.

CHICKEN LITTLE

2 slices whole wheat bread

4 slices sharp cheddar cheese

3 slices bacon

Light drizzle of honey mustard

Chicken salad*, to taste

* To make the chicken salad, combine boiled chicken, celery, three parts mayo, and one part honey, then season with salt and pepper.

STEP 1: Grease one side of each slice of bread and place in a pan on medium heat, greased side down. Place the cheese on the bread so that all of the bread is covered.

STEP 2: Put the bacon on one slice of bread.

STEP 3: Drizzle the honey mustard over the cheese.

STEP 4: Once the cheese is melted, put the chicken salad onto the cheese.

STEP 5: Put both halves together and take a big ol' bite.

PAIRING

A nice malty Oktoberfest style beer will keep you from thinking the sky is falling. **Spaten's Oktoberfest** is a safe bet, but **Hofbräu** is always solid.

DRAGON BALL CHEESE

1 Pita bread

Handful of soba noodles

⅓ pound cubed roasted pork

1 shredded carrot

¼ pound queso fresco

Sriracha (or your favorite hot sauce), to taste

STEP 1: Open the pita bread and hollow it out.

STEP 2: Fill with noodles, then pork, sriracha, carrot, and queso fresco.

STEP 3: Place in an oven or toaster oven at 350°F for 5-6 minutes, or until the cheese is nice and melted.

STEP 4: Take out of the oven and enjoy.

PAIRING

With a little bit of Asian flavor and a fiery sriracha note, we could only think about the Z Fighters. You're going to want something refreshing to pair with this sandwich. **Sapporo** is the drink of choice with this one. KAAAMEEEHAAA-MEEE…YUM!!!!

SO LONG AND THANKS FOR ALL THE TUNA FISH

Tuna fish

½ spoonful Dijon mustard

½ spoonful horseradish

1 sweet gherkin pickle, diced

2 slices multi-grain bread

1 spoonful mayonnaise

2 slices best aged cheddar cheese you can find (preferably 10 years)

2 slices provolone cheese

1 slice tomato

STEP 1: Mix the tuna, mustard, horseradish, and diced pickle.

STEP 2: Grease one side of each slice of bread with mayonnaise and place in a pan on medium heat, greased side down. One piece should be covered with tuna salad and cheddar, the other with provolone and one slice of tomato.

STEP 3: Place in the oven until melted.

STEP 4: Don't panic.

STEP 5: Combine and enjoy.

PAIRING

Ideally, we'd have you pair this one with a Pan-Galactic Gargle Blaster. It is the best drink in the galaxy, after all. But if you can't find one in your travels, any nice IPA will do. **Driftwood Brewery's Fat Tug IPA** will be a nice hoppy complement to a galactic classic. And if IPAs aren't your thing, try **Driftwood Brewery's White Bark Ale** for a nice wheat alternative.

EXPERT

YOU'VE REALLY
CAUGHT ON QUICK,
WE'RE PROUD OF YOU

LEAF EATER

3–5 broccoli florets
Handful of spinach
1 good-sized piece ciabatta bread
4 slices fresh mozzarella
3 slices tomato
Balsamic vinegar, to drizzle

STEP 1: Steam the broccoli and spinach in a pan on medium heat, until tender.

STEP 2: Slice the ciabatta in half and drizzle the balsamic vinegar on the bread.

STEP 3: Put the fresh mozzarella slices on the ciabatta and the tomato slices on top of the mozzarella.

STEP 4: Put the steamed broccoli and spinach on top of the tomatoes.

STEP 5: Put both halves of in an oven or toaster oven at 350°F for 5 minutes.

STEP 6: Take both halves out of the oven and slap them together. Pat yourself on the back for eating healthy and enjoy your Leaf Eater.

PAIRING

Who needs meat? Beer complements greens just as well as bacon. So for those meat-challenged of you out there, we recommend something light and refreshing to let those veggies announce their arrival. Any kind of wheat will do, and **Flying Dog's In-Heat Wheat** is a standout. Its fruity and spicy nature is a perfect complement for all those leaves wrapped in melty goodness. It's a combo worthy of next year's Arbor Day party.

97

JALAPEÑO POPPER

2 slices white bread
1 batch of beer batter*
2 sliced jalapeño peppers
Cream cheese, to taste

*To make a simple and easy beer batter, combine 2 cups of self-rising flour and 1 can or bottle of your favorite beer and whisk together until combined.

STEP 1: Dip the slices of white bread in the beer batter.

STEP 2: Put both slices of bread in a pan on medium heat and cook for 1–2 minutes, or until bread starts to brown.

STEP 3: Flip the bread and spread a generous amount of cream cheese on the cooked side of the bread.

STEP 4: Put the sliced jalapeño peppers onto the cream cheese.

STEP 5: When the cream cheese is soft, put both slices together and hot damn, you've got yourself a Jalapeño Popper sandwich.

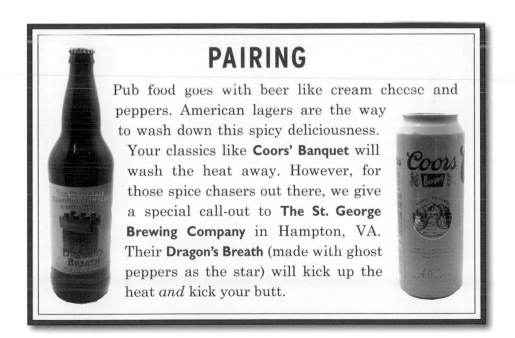

PAIRING

Pub food goes with beer like cream cheese and peppers. American lagers are the way to wash down this spicy deliciousness. Your classics like **Coors' Banquet** will wash the heat away. However, for those spice chasers out there, we give a special call-out to **The St. George Brewing Company** in Hampton, VA. Their **Dragon's Breath** (made with ghost peppers as the star) will kick up the heat *and* kick your butt.

TRUFFLE SHUFFLE

3 thin slices ham
2 slices whole grain bread
6 thin slices Italian truffle cheese
Truffle oil, to drizzle

STEP 1: In a pan on medium heat, lightly grill the ham.

STEP 2: Grease one side of each slice of bread and place in a pan on medium heat, greased side down.

STEP 3: Put the truffle cheese on the bread so that all of the bread is covered.

STEP 4: Put the grilled ham on top of the truffle cheese.

STEP 5: Very lightly drizzle the truffle oil over the ham.

STEP 6: When the cheese is melted, put both slices together and enjoy.

PAIRING

From the whole grain bread to the truffles, this one screams earthy notes. To accentuate that nutty earth flavor, you're gonna need some equally muted and malty flavors. It's hard to outshine a truffle, so it's probably in your best interest to complement it as best as possible. Any English nut brown will do a nice, subtle job, but for those looking to give the truffle a little run for its money, one of the more flavorful European pilsners would do the trick. **Pilsner Urquell** is a perfect partner for this pig-found nugget.

SUPER MARIO BRUSCHETTA

1 piece focaccia bread
4 slices Asiago cheese
¼ pound bruschetta
Handful of chopped mushrooms
2 leaves basil

STEP 1: Slice the focaccia in half, cover with Asiago cheese, and put them in the oven.

STEP 2: After a minute or so, put the bruschetta on the bottom half of the bread.

STEP 3: In a pan, sauté the chopped mushrooms.

STEP 4: When the cheese is melted on the focaccia, take it out of the oven and put the basil leaves on the top half.

STEP 5: Place the sautéed mushroom on top of the bruschetta.

STEP 6: Put it together and enjoy your Super Mario Bruschetta while you beat Bowser.

PAIRING

Based solely on the name, we want to suggest **Ithaca Beer Company's Flower Power**. Get it? Because of the fire flowers in Super Mario Brothers…? The hoppy backbone will balance nicely with the Asiago and earthy mushrooms. Let's a-go!

GRILLED CHEESE –IT'S WHAT'S FOR BREAKFAST

2 eggs
2 slices white bread
4 slices American cheese
2 strips bacon
Handful of shredded cheddar cheese
Maple syrup, to drizzle

STEP 1: In a pan on medium heat, cook both eggs so that they are over-easy.

STEP 2: Grease one side of each slice of bread and place in a pan on medium heat, greased side down

STEP 3: Put the American cheese on the bread so that all of the bread is covered.

STEP 4: On one slice of bread, put both strips of bacon. On the other slice, put one of the over-easy eggs.

STEP 5: Drizzle maple syrup over both slices of bread.

STEP 6: When the cheese is melted, put both slices together.

STEP 7: Sprinkle shredded cheddar on top of the sandwich and place the second over-easy egg on top of the cheddar. Cut the sandwich in half and enjoy (you may want to bring some napkins because it's gonna be messy).

PAIRING

You want something hearty and robust to complement the complicated flavors that are created by maple syrup, eggs, and cheddar. Like our other breakfast offering (The Bee's Knees), a breakfast stout will do the trick for this one. If you're looking to replicate a breakfast classic, try **Joe Mama's Milk** coffee stout from **Keegan Ales**.

PESTO CHANGO

4 slices eggplant
1 good-sized piece ciabatta bread
1 spoonful pesto
4 slices mozzarella cheese
3 slices roasted red peppers

STEP 1: Grill the eggplant slices until soft.

STEP 2: Slice the ciabatta in half and spread the pesto on both halves.

STEP 3: Put the mozzarella on both slices so that all of the bread is completely covered.

STEP 4: Put the roasted red pepper slices and eggplant on top of the cheese.

STEP 5: Put both halves in an oven or toaster oven at 350°F for 4–5 minutes, or until the cheese is melted.

STEP 6: Take both halves out of the oven, put them together, and *abracadabra* you've got yourself a Pesto Chango.

PAIRING

A nice pilsner is a great, refreshing pairing for this one. **Pilsner Urquell** is a classic, but if you're looking to go with something that matches purely on name alone, **Magic Hat's Hocus Pocus** is just magical.

DIA DE LOS QUESOS

1 chicken cutlet

2 tortillas

Handful of shredded cheddar cheese

3 slices cheddar cheese

3 slices pepper jack cheese

1 spoonful salsa (choose your favorite)

1 sliced jalapeño pepper

Salt and pepper, to taste

STEP 1: Cut the chicken cutlet into strips and grill (lightly season with salt and pepper).

STEP 2: Put the first tortilla in a pan on medium heat, and then cover with shredded cheddar.

STEP 3: When the cheese on the first tortilla is starting to melt, put the second tortilla on top of the first and cover in cheddar and pepper jack.

STEP 4: On half of the tortilla, put the grilled chicken strips, jalapeño slices, and salsa.

STEP 5: Carefully fold the tortilla in half and cook on both sides until both are golden brown.

STEP 6: Take the tortillas out of the pan cut into four pieces, and get ready to take on the Dia de los Quesos.

PAIRING

Okay, sure, we know what you're thinking. But a quesadilla is *totally* a grilled cheese. For sure. And like the deserts in which such a delicious concoction was probably founded (we don't really know where), it needs something cool and refreshing to fight back the spices. For the sake of solidarity, a **Negra Modelo** has the malty flavor to counteract the spices, and its older more popular brother, **Modelo Especial**, has the refreshing lager taste to bring your taste buds back down to earth. Really, there is a reason that most Mexican and Caribbean beers are super refreshing. Their food is spicy. Super spicy. So feel free to get *loco* with this one.

THE NATURE BOY RICOTTA FLAIR

2 slices whole wheat bread

1 spoonful ricotta cheese

3 basil leaves

2 halves roasted red peppers

Handful of spinach

Balsamic vinaigrette, to drizzle

STEP 1: Grease one side of each slice of bread and place in a pan on medium heat, greased side down.

STEP 2: Lightly spread ricotta on the bread so that all of the bread is covered.

STEP 3: When the bread starts to turn golden brown, put the basil, roasted red peppers, and spinach on the bread.

STEP 4: Drizzle balsamic vinaigrette over the sandwich.

STEP 5: When the bread is golden brown, take it out of the pan, slice, and enjoy.

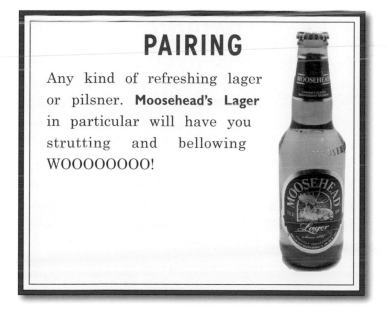

PAIRING

Any kind of refreshing lager or pilsner. **Moosehead's Lager** in particular will have you strutting and bellowing WOOOOOOOO!

THE TWILIGHT PROVOLONE

6 slices provolone cheese
1 good-sized piece ciabatta bread
2 halves roasted red peppers
¼ pound roast beef
1 egg

STEP 1: Put three slices of provolone on each half of the ciabatta.

STEP 2: On one half of the ciabatta, put the roasted red peppers and then add the roast beef on top of the peppers.

STEP 3: Put both halves in an oven at 350°F until the cheese is melted.

STEP 4: While the ciabatta is in the oven, fry one egg over-easy in a frying pan.

STEP 5: When the cheese on the ciabatta is melted, take both halves out of the oven and place the over-easy egg on top of the roast beef.

STEP 6: Put the sandwich together, slice, and enjoy.

PAIRING

Prepare to enter the Twilight Provolone. We'd planned to recreate the epic intro to our favorite genre classic, but then we thought about copyright infringement and all of the drama that comes with it. So, instead of respectfully plagiarizing your favorite TV shows, try this one with an off-kilter beer. Take a step back in time and over into another dimension and pick up **Dogfish Head's Midas Touch**, a recreation of an ancient beer found in King Midas' tomb.

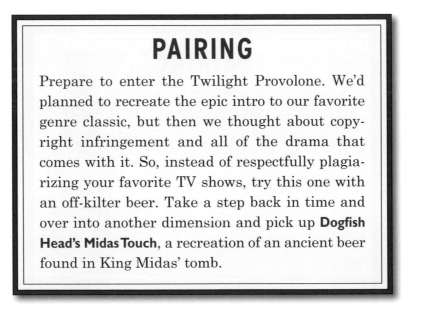

PITA PITA PESTO EATA

1 pita bread
1 spoonful pesto
¼ pound pancetta
Handful of spinach
¼ chopped tomato
Handful of shredded cheddar cheese

STEP 1: Hollow out the pita bread so that it forms a pouch.

STEP 2: Spread the pesto so that it evenly covers the inside of the pita.

STEP 3: Roughly chop the pancetta.

STEP 4: In a bowl, mix together the spinach, chopped tomato, pancetta, and shredded cheddar.

STEP 5: Stuff the pita with the mixture and place in oven at 350°F.

STEP 6: When the cheese is melted, take it out of the oven and enjoy.

PAIRING

Like the Leaf Eater (page 97), this one begs for something refreshing. Go for a lager or hefeweizen. We'd even recommend mixing a **Hefeweizen** with some banana nectar. Banana weizens are delicioso!

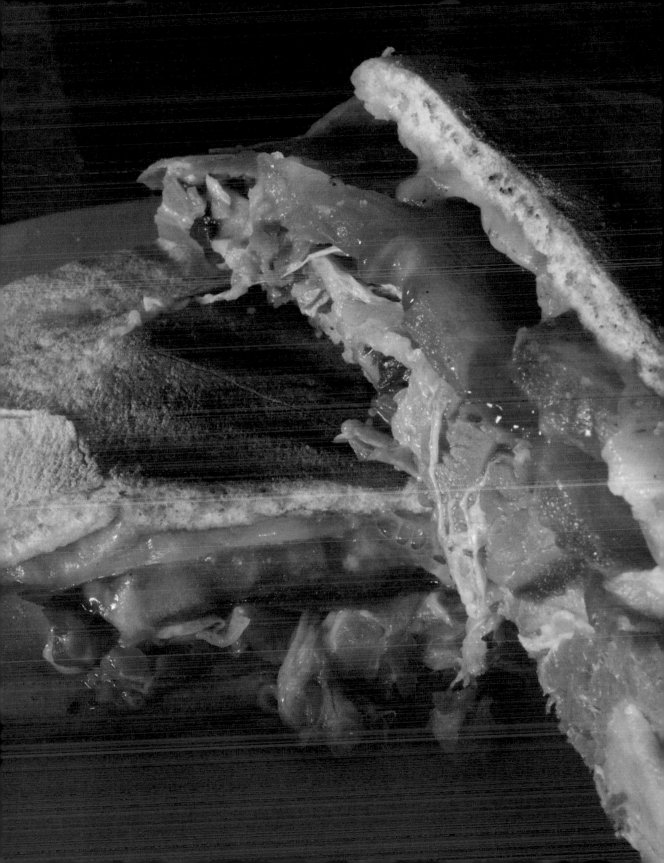

OUT FOR ASPARAGUS

2 slices sourdough bread
2 slices goat cheese
Grilled asparagus
2 artichoke hearts
I roasted red pepper
4 slices grilled eggplant
Oil and vinegar, to drizzle

STEP 1: Grease one side of each slice of bread and place in a pan on medium heat, and then cover the bread in goat cheese.

STEP 2: Cut the asparagus shoots in half and begin to fry in separate pan.

STEP 3: Put the artichoke hearts in the pan with the asparagus and cook until everything starts to brown.

STEP 4: Put the artichoke and asparagus onto one side of the bread.

STEP 5: Put the roasted red pepper and grilled eggplant on the other side of the bread and drizzle with oil and vinegar.

STEP 6: Put both halves together and have a bite of Out for Asparagus.

PAIRING

We recommend an **American Lager** to let this one shine. It'll have you happier than Sega when he finally finds justice.

HARD TO GRILL

2 slices whole grain bread

4 slices Taleggio cheese

Mushrooms and onions

Handful of mixed greens

¼ pound turkey

¼ avocado

Spicy Dijon mustard, to drizzle

STEP 1: Grease one side of each slice of bread and place in a pan on medium heat, then cover with the Taleggio.

STEP 2: In a separate pan, sauté the mushrooms and onions.

STEP 3: In a third pan, lightly grill the turkey.

STEP 4: Drizzle spicy Dijon mustard over the cheese.

STEP 5: Put the sautéed mushrooms, onions, mixed greens, and grilled turkey onto the bread.

STEP 6: Put both halves together, sit back, and enjoy your sandwich while watching a Steven Seagal movie and remember that he is Hard to Grill.

PAIRING

Somebody must have been watching a Seagal marathon while writing these recipes. Two references to the ponytailed master of street justice might be two too many, but here we are. Try a **Samuel Adams' Nitro White Ale**. It's super refreshing and the use of nitrogen will give it a mouth feel, as the nitrogen uses smaller bubbles than CO_2. It makes this combo kind of tough to beat... and hard to grill.

LORD OF THE WASTELAND HUMMUS

2 spicy Italian sausages
1 pita bread
6 ounces goat cheese
1 spoonful hummus
Handful of kale

STEP 1: Cut the sausages in half and cook.

STEP 2: Hollow out the pita bread and put half of the goat cheese on the bottom, followed by the hummus, kale, cooked sausage, and the rest of the goat cheese.

STEP 3: Put in an oven at 350°F until the goat cheese is hot and melty.

STEP 4: Take out of the oven and enjoy.

PAIRING

We worked really hard to get a *Mad Max* reference in here. Many may not pick up on it, but at least we got it in. We like a dark beer to accentuate the strong flavors. **Founders' Backwoods Bastard** is a bourbon dark beer. It's limited, just like justice in the Thunder Dome. So get it when you can.

SHO 'NUFF

1 batch of beer batter*

4 pickle slices

2 slices potato bread

4 slices sharp cheddar cheese

Handful of kale

Ranch dressing, to drizzle

2 cups self rising flour and a can/bottle of beer, vegetable oil

* To make a simple and easy beer batter, combine 2 cups of self-rising flour and 1 can or bottle of your favorite beer and whisk together until combined.

STEP 1: Dip the pickle slices into the beer batter and fry in vegetable oil. Set aside.

STEP 2: Grease one side of each slice of bread and place in a pan on medium heat, and then cover with cheddar.

STEP 3: When the cheddar starts to melt, put the fried pickles and kale on the bread.

STEP 4: Drizzle ranch on both slices of bread.

STEP 5: Put the sandwich together and take a bite of the baddest, most low-down sandwich in town, Sho 'Nuff.

PAIRING

Eddie loves *The Last Dragon*. As he says, "It's pretty much *Big Trouble in Little China*, except in Harlem, and starring a guy who looks like Prince." You need strong flavors to complement this one properly. Without a good partner, this sandwich will kung-fu you up. So try it with a bock beer. **Shiner Bock** is pretty easy to find and suitably robust.

THE SUPER ITALIAN STALLION

1 ½ cups Italian bread crumbs

4 eggs

2 slices white bread

3 slices mozzarella cheese

3 slices provolone cheese

⅛ pound capicola

⅛ pound prosciutto

⅛ pound soppressata

1 onion

Oil and vinegar, to taste

2 banana peppers

2 sun-dried tomatoes

Oil and vinegar, to taste

STEP 1: In a bowl, put bread crumbs and in a separate bowl, crack four eggs.

STEP 2: Dip the bread in egg, and then bread crumbs. Grease a pan and place the bread in the pan.

STEP 3: When one side of the bread starts to brown, flip the bread and cover the top with both cheeses.

STEP 4: Lightly fry the capicola, prosciutto, soppressata, and onions, then drizzle with oil and vinegar.

STEP 5: Once the cheese starts to melt, put the banana peppers and sun-dried tomatoes on one side of the bread.

STEP 6: On the other side of the bread, put the fried capicola, prosciutto, soppressata, and onions.

STEP 7: Put the sandwich together, pop in a Rocky movie, and enjoy the Super Italian Stallion.

PAIRING

The man was just nominated for an Oscar…for the same role he won for eight films ago. So show some respect. We recommend **Peroni** lager to let this combo go all "first blood" on your taste buds. That's a good thing, just like the movie.

GLEAMING THE BRIE

1 wedge brie
2 slices sourdough bread
Handful of fresh raspberries
1 spoonful chocolate chips
1 spoonful blackberry preserves
Honey, to drizzle

STEP 1: Cut the brie into six slices.

STEP 2: Grease one side of each slice of bread and place in a pan on medium heat, then cover in brie slices.

STEP 3: When the brie starts to melt, spread the blackberry preserves over the bread.

STEP 4: Sprinkle the raspberries and chocolate chips over the preserves, and then drizzle honey over the entire sandwich.

STEP 5: When the brie is fully melted, carefully slap both slices together, slice, and enjoy.

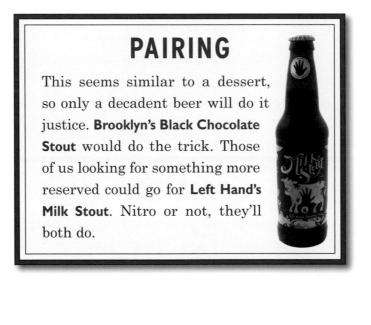

PAIRING

This seems similar to a dessert, so only a decadent beer will do it justice. **Brooklyn's Black Chocolate Stout** would do the trick. Those of us looking for something more reserved could go for **Left Hand's Milk Stout**. Nitro or not, they'll both do.

ASIAGO YOU WISH

2 slices sourdough bread
4 slices Asiago cheese
Handful of kale
1 spoonful pepper jelly
¼ pound pancetta

STEP 1: Grease one side of each slice of bread and place in a pan on medium heat, greased side down. Place the cheese on the bread so that all of the bread is covered.

STEP 2: In a separate pan, steam the kale and place on one slice of the bread.

STEP 3: On the other slice of bread, spread the pepper jelly.

STEP 4: Put the pancetta on top of the kale.

STEP 5: Once the cheese is melted, put both halves together and enjoy it Asiago You Wish.

PAIRING

Grab a hoppy IPA for this one. **Founders' All Day IPA** will make for a delicious pairing. Your wish is our command.

HOT POTATO

2 boiled red skin potatoes

1 sprig rosemary

Drizzle of olive oil

1 large biscuit

2 slices provolone cheese

¼ pound roasted chicken (or just grab a rotisserie chicken from your local grocery store)

Gravy (homemade or just grab an easy gravy packet)

STEP 1: Chop the potatoes into large chunks, then place in a pan and cover with rosemary and olive oil. Cover with foil, and then put in an oven or toaster oven at 350°F for 10 minutes.

STEP 2: When the potatoes are done, cut the biscuit in half, cover with provolone and put the potatoes on the bottom half. Put in the oven at 350°F.

STEP 3: Heat the chicken in a pan.

STEP 4: Once the cheese is melted on the biscuit, take it out of the oven and put the chicken on the potatoes, then drizzle gravy over the whole sandwich.

STEP 5: Put the top on the sandwich and chop it in half. Take a bite and watch the Jim Kelly movie this tasty one is named after.

PAIRING

These flavors are basic, unlike Jim Kelly's sweet karate moves, so something with a nice hop backbone is what's needed. Try out **Sixpoint Brewery's Bengali Tiger**. This American IPA will make you want to twist the tiger's tail. Go ahead, we dare you.

BACON ME CRAZY

2 slices sourdough bread
5 slices cheddar cheese
6 slices raw bacon

STEP 1: Put the slices of cheddar in between the sourdough.

STEP 2: Put both slices of bread together and wrap in raw bacon slices, in a lattice pattern.

STEP 3: Put the bacon-wrapped sandwich in a pan on medium heat.

STEP 4: Carefully flip the sandwich every 1–2 minutes, until the bacon is mostly cooked.

STEP 5: Carefully take the sandwich out of the pan, cut it in half, and hold on tight because this one is a doozy (you might want to use a knife and fork).

PAIRING

Only one beer comes to our minds when we think of this behemoth. **Stone Brewery's Arrogant Bastard** is the only beer that makes sense with this one. Nobody in their right mind can go into this one thinking it's going to be as delicious as it is. That's because it's too good for you. The flavors are too complex and layered for your brain to properly process. The human brain is not designed to deal with this much awesomeness at one time. Enjoy.

BEYOND PROVOLONE

3 slices sourdough bread
8 slices provolone cheese
2 pineapple rings
⅛ pound prosciutto
3 slices pickled beets

STEP 1: Grease one side of all three slices of sourdough and place in a pan on medium heat, then cover with the provolone.

STEP 2: In another pan, grill the pineapple rings.

STEP 3: When the cheese is melted, split the prosciutto between two slices of the bread.

STEP 4: On one slice of bread with prosciutto, put the slices of beet.

STEP 5: On the other slice of bread with prosciutto, put the grilled pineapple.

STEP 6: Stack the slices of bread with the prosciutto/beets slice on the bottom, then the slice with just provolone, and finally the slice with prosciutto and pineapple.

STEP 7: Slice the sandwich and enjoy.

PAIRING

Yes! Another *Mad Max* sandy! A nice IPA will make you feel like the road warrior himself. Try **Stone Brewery's IPA**. We love *Mad Max*. Get over it. George Miller also made *Babe* and *Happy Feet*…they're also good.

ROCKY HORROR CHEESE SHOW

4 eggs

2 slices challah bread

4 slices turkey

3 slices Gouda cheese

2 slices onion

4 thin slices Swiss cheese

Drizzle of Thousand Island dressing

5 olives

1 spoonful crumbled Gruyère cheese

STEP 1: Crack the eggs into a bowl and whisk until blended, then dip the challah bread in the egg mixture.

STEP 2: Butter a pan and lightly fry one side of each slice of challah bread.

STEP 3: Lightly grill the turkey and melt the Gouda on top.

STEP 4: Flip the challah bread and cover in onions and Swiss cheese.

STEP 5: Put the turkey and melted Gouda on the Swiss cheese and top with Thousand Island dressing and olives.

STEP 6: Put the slices of bread together and top with Gruyère. Now comes the end of the ANTICI…PATION! You can now enter the Rocky Horror Cheese Show.

PAIRING

Samuel Smith's Oatmeal Stout will complement the nice breakfast notes while maintaining the flavor combination and, you know, do the time warp and all that jazz.

THE SWEET TREAT

4 eggs

½ tablespoon vanilla extract

1 Hawaiian roll

Sweetened cream cheese*

4 sliced strawberries

1 handful of blueberries

1 spoonful chocolate chips

Powdered cinnamon, to taste

* To make sweetened cream cheese, combine 24 ounces of cream cheese, ¾ cup of sugar, a few drops of vanilla extract, and 2 cups of heavy cream and mix until smooth.

STEP 1: Crack the eggs in a bowl and add a few drops of vanilla extract, then whisk until blended and dip the Hawaiian roll in the egg mixture.

STEP 2: Butter a pan and lightly fry one side of each slice of the Hawaiian roll

STEP 3: When one side of the roll starts to brown, flip it over and fry the other side.

STEP 4: After the roll is flipped, spread the sweetened cream cheese on both sides of the roll.

STEP 5: Put the strawberries, blueberries, and chocolate chips on the sweetened cream cheese.

STEP 6: When the other side of the roll is brown, put the sandwich together, take it out of the pan, and sprinkle with powdered cinnamon.

STEP 7: Plop it in on a plate with a side of sweetened cream cheese for dipping, and get lost in The Sweet Treat.

PAIRING

Lake Placid makes a delightful vanilla porter called **Black Tie**, but it's super limited by region and season. So try **Goose Island's Bourbon County barrel aged stout**. It's decadent for different reasons, but still pretty dang awesome.

THE HAM OF LA CHALLAH

5 eggs
2 slices challah bread
6 slices grilled ham
Handful of spinach
Handful of bean sprouts
Sun-dried tomato cream cheese,
    to taste

STEP 1: Crack four eggs into a bowl and whisk until blended, and then dip the challah bread in the egg mixture.

STEP 2: Butter a pan and lightly fry one side of each slice of the challah bread.

STEP 3: In a separate pan, lightly grill the ham.

STEP 4: When the challah bread starts to brown, flip it over and spread the sun-dried tomato cream cheese on both sides.

STEP 5: Put the grilled ham, spinach, and bean sprouts onto the cream cheese.

STEP 6: When the other side of the challah bread starts to brown, close up the sandwich.

STEP 7: In a separate pan, fry one over-easy egg and place it on top of the sandwich.

STEP 8: Cut the sandwich in half and taste The Ham of La Challah.

PAIRING

This reference is obscure. We're sorry about that. This grilled cheese needs something a little on the lighter side, perhaps an American or European lager. But if you're feeling adventurous, try one of the many Gose's available today. The German-style sour beer makes a good counter to those refreshing ingredients. **Anderson Valley Brewing Company** makes a fantastic **Briney Melon Gose**.

NACHO LIBERTE

Handful of tortilla chips

4 eggs

2 slices white bread

1 batch of homemade Corona
    cheese dip*

1 sliced jalapeño

*To make the cheese dip, use 1 bottle
    of Corona, 8 ounces of shredded
    cheddar, and 8 ounces of cream
    cheese (cubed). In a saucepan, pour
    the bottle of corona and let simmer,
    then add the cheddar and cream
    cheese and stir until combined.

STEP 1: In a bowl, crush the tortilla chips. In a separate bowl, crack four eggs.

STEP 2: Dip the bread in egg, then the chips. Grease a pan and place the bread in the pan.

STEP 3: When one side of the bread starts to brown, flip to the other side.

STEP 4: Spread the cheese dip and jalapeños over the bread.

STEP 5: When the other side of the bread starts to brown and crisp, take it out of the pan and slap that bad boy together.

PAIRING

To commemorate Jack Black's finest performance, we recommend something light with flavor to go with this one. **Sierra Nevada's IPA** has enough hop character to balance the spice nicely. Their new tropical release will add a different dimension.

CHEESE LOUISE...AND GENE...AND TINA

¼ pound ground beef
⅛ chopped onion
1 tablespoon minced garlic
4 eggs
1 hamburger bun
4 slices American cheese
1 spoonful coleslaw
2 whole pickles
Ketchup, to drizzle

STEP 1: In a bowl, mix the ground beef, onion, minced garlic, and two scrambled eggs, then shape into a patty.

STEP 2: In a pan, fry the beef patty.

STEP 3: When the patty is almost cooked, grease the bun and place face-down in a separate pan.

STEP 4: When the bun is lightly grilled, flip and cover in cheese.

STEP 5: When the burger is done, take it out of the pan and place on the bun. Then take the other two eggs and scramble and cook them.

STEP 6: On top of the burger, put the coleslaw and pickles.

STEP 7: Put the scrambled eggs on top of the burger, and then drizzle with ketchup.

STEP 8: Put the whole together, then sit down and take a bite of a burger that Bob himself would be proud of.

PAIRING

So yeah, this is a big one. As anyone with cable, Netflix, or Hulu has probably guessed by now, *Bob's Burgers* was (and still is) a pretty big influence for us. The biggest. So we hope this one does it justice. We'd like to imagine that Bob's a pretty traditional guy and drinks traditional beer. **Flying Dog's Doggy Style** classic pale ale fits the bill. We hope Bob would approve.

BIG BREAKFAST IN LITTLE SANDWICH

½ red pepper
2 sausage links
2 slices challah bread
2 slices cheddar cheese
2 slices mozzarella cheese
2 eggs
4 apple slices
2 slices tomato
Maple syrup, to drizzle

STEP 1: Chop the pepper and cut the sausage links in half, then fry them together.

STEP 2: Grease one side of each slice of bread and place in a pan on medium heat, then cover each slice of bread with one slice of cheddar and one slice of mozzarella.

STEP 3: In a separate pan, fry both eggs over-easy and set aside.

STEP 4: Place the apple and tomato slices on one slice of bread.

STEP 5: Put the fried peppers and sausage on the other slice of bread.

STEP 6: Put both over-easy eggs on top of the peppers and sausage, then drizzle maple syrup over everything (go nuts…the more, the better).

STEP 7: When the cheese is melted, quickly but gently place the slice with tomato and apples on top of the eggs.

STEP 8: Slice it in half, watch it ooze in all the right ways, and take a step into the magic that is Big Breakfast in Little Sandwich.

PAIRING

We think Kurt Russell would approve. We hope to ask him one day. Try this one with a nice, refreshing wheat beer. The go-to's are **Blue Moon** or **Shock Top**, because they're everywhere. But try and find a **Hacker-Pschorr** or **Weihenstephaner** and you won't be sorry.

EPILOGUE

We hope you've enjoyed this little malt- and dairy-fueled escapade as much as we have. This book has been a dream come true for Eddie and myself. What started with a dream and an off-handed comment to a fellow lifeguard has now manifested itself into something we think is pretty special, and we hope that you do, too!

So we want to thank you. To the avid used bookstore patron and the lover of obscure cookbooks: we thank you! And to the college senior and beer snobs who've just finished the first chapter of *American Sour Beers*: cheers to you guys!

Without all of you, we couldn't have checked this box on our list of life goals. And hey, you never know, there could be more to come. We sure hope there is. So spread the word because we'd like to think the best is yet to come. But for now, as we go back to the drawing board to concoct some new delicious ideas, we hope that we've inspired you to come up with some of your own. We can, however, paraphrase Hawkeye (Hawk Guy?) and say, "Captain, it's been our genuine pleasure." To write for you guys, that is. Prost, Salut, Egészségére, and most importantly,

Cheers!!

KEVIN VANBLARCUM

Born and raised in the Catskill Mountains, Kevin currently resides in Pine Hill, New York where he works as a brewer and writer. After graduating from the University at Albany, he began pursuing a career in the brewing industry. He shares his life with his loving fiancé, Cassie, and their cat, Egg.

JAMES EDWARD DAVIS

Originally from Washington D.C., Eddie moved to upstate New York to attend SUNY Delhi.

Along the way, he fell in love with the culinary arts and began to hone his skills at a local favorite, The Caboose. A skating fanatic and movie buff, he currently resides in Brooklyn where the pavement is less bumpy.

RECIPE INDEX

RECIPE INDEX